SONGS GALORE

SONGS GALORE

by

COLIN McKAY

A collection of songs for community and camp-fire singing by Scouts, Guides, Youth Organisations, and adult groups.

GLASGOW

BROWN, SON & FERGUSON, LTD.

4-10 DARNLEY STREET, G41 2SD

First Edition 1982

ISBN 0 85174 428 1

Printed and made in Great Britain

To Shirley . . . .

who every day brings the joy of song into my life.

CONTENTS

Contents—cont.

SHORT SONGS AND ROUNDS

Contents—cont.

SONGS WITH ACTIONS

Contents—cont.

FOLK SONGS AND SPIRITUALS

CLOSING SONGS

Contents—cont.

PAGE

OPENING SONGS

COMING UP THE VALLEY

We're coming up the valley, coming up the valley,
Coming up the valley, one by one, one by one.
We're coming up the valley, coming up the valley,
Coming to the rising of the sun.

(*Repeat 3 times. Singing should start quietly and get louder and louder*).

We're going down the valley, going down the valley,
Going down the valley, one by one, one by one.
We're going down the valley, going down the valley,
Going to the setting of the sun.

(*Repeat 3 times. Singing should start loudly and get quieter and quieter*).

THE MORE WE GET TOGETHER

The more we get together, together, together,
The more we get together, the merrier we will be,
For your friends are my friends,
And my friends are your friends,
The more we get together, the merrier we will be.

The more we get together, together, together,
The more we get together, the merrier we will be,
For you know that I know,
And I know that you know,
The more we get together, the merrier we will be.

WELCOME

(*Tune:* Auld Lang Syne)

We welcome you to our camp-fire,
We are very pleased you came,
To join with us and sing aloud,
The glories of our game.

We thank you for your presence here,
Our camp-fire to enjoy,
We greet you well, we wish you well,
From every man and boy.

TONIGHT'S THE NIGHT

(*Tune:* Auld Lang Syne)

Tonight's the night for fun and games,
A rousing song or two,
Around the campfires roaring glow,
There's a place for you and me.

Draw near, a yarn I'll tell you now,
Of spurs that have been won,
And song and sketch will warm your hearts,
Before this night is done.

GENERAL SONGS

ON ILKLA MOOR BAHT 'AT

Wheer 'as tha bin sin I saw thee?
On Ilkla Moor baht 'at.
Wheer 'as tha bin sin I saw thee?
Wheer 'as tha bin sin I saw thee?

(*Chorus*) On Ilkla Moor baht 'at,
On Ilkla Moor baht 'at,
On Ilkla Moor baht 'at.

Tha's bin a-coourtin' Mary Jane,
On Ilkla Moor baht 'at.
Tha's bin a-courtin' Mary Jane,
Tha's bin a-courtin' Mary Jane.

(*Chorus*) On Ilkla Moor baht 'at . . . . . .

Tha'll surely catch thy death o' cowld,
On Ilkla Moor baht 'at.
Tha'll surely catch thy death o' cowld,
Tha'll surely catch thy death o' cowld.

(*Chorus*) On Ilkla Moor baht 'at . . . . . .

Then we shall ha' ta' bury thee,
On Ilkla Moor baht 'at.
Then we shall ha' ta' bury thee,
Then we shall ha' ta' bury thee.

(*Chorus*) On Ilkla Moor baht 'at . . . . . .

Then worms'll coom an' ate thee oop,
On Ilkla Moor baht 'at.
Then worms'll coom an' ate thee oop,
Then worms'll coom an' ate thee oop.

(*Chorus*) On Ilkla Moor baht 'at . . . . . .

Then docks'll coom an' ate oop worms,
On Ilkla Moor baht 'at.
Then dooks'll coom an' ate oop worms,
Then dooks'll coom an' ate oop worms.

(*Chorus*) On Ilkla Moor baht 'at . . . . . .

Then we shall coom an' ate oop dooks,
On Ilkla Moor baht 'at.
Then we shall coom an' ate oop dooks,
Then we shall coom an' ate oop dooks.

(*Chorus*) On Ilkla Moor baht 'at . . . . . .

Then we shall all 'av etten thee,
On Ilkla Moor baht 'at.
Then we shall all 'av etten thee,
Then we shall all 'av etten thee.

(*Chorus*) On Ilkla Moor baht 'at . . . . . .

OLD FOLKS AT HOME

'Way down upon the Swanee river,
Far, far away,
There's where my heart is turning ever,
There's where the old folks stay.
All up and down the old creation
Sadly I roam,
Still looking for the old plantation
And for the old folks at home.

(*Chorus*) All the world is sad and dreary,
Ev'rywhere I roam.
Oh! darkies, how my heart grows weary,
Far from the old folks at home.

All round the little farm I wandered
When I was young;
Then many happy days I squandered,
Many the songs I sung.
When I was playing with my brother
Happy was I.
Oh! take me to my kind old mother,
There let me live and die!

(*Chorus*) All the world . . . . . .

SWING LOW, SWEET CHARIOT

I looked over Jordan an' what did I see
Comin' for to carry me home!
A band of angels comin' after me
Comin' for to carry me home.

(*Chorus*) Swing low, sweet chariot
Comin' for to carry me home!
Swing low, sweet chariot
Comin' for to carry me home!

If you get there before I do,
Comin' for to carry me home,
Jess tell my frien's that I'm a-comin' too,
Comin' for to carry me home.

(*Chorus*) Swing low . . . . . .

SWEET AND LOW

Sweet and low, sweet and low,
Wind of the western sea;
Low, low breathe and blow,
Wind of the western sea;
Over the rolling waters go,
Come from the dying moon and blow,
Blow him again to me;
While my little one, while my pretty one sleeps.

Sleep and rest, sleep and rest,
Father will come to thee soon;
Rest, rest on mother's breast,
Father will come to thee soon;
Father will come to his babe in the nest,
Silver sails all out of the west.
Under the silver moon,
Sleep, my little one, sleep, my pretty one, sleep.

POLLY WOLLY DOODLE

Oh, I went down South for to see my Sal,
Singing Polly Wolly Doodle all the day.
Oh, my Sal she am a dandy gal,
Singing Polly Wolly Doodle all the day.

(*Chorus*) Fare thee well! Fare thee well!
Fare thee well my fairy fay!
Oh, I'm off to Louisiana,
For to see my Susy Anna,
Singing Polly Wolly Doodle all the day.

Oh, my Sal she am a maiden fair,
Singing Polly Wolly Doodle all the day.
With laughing eyes and curly hair,
Singing Polly Wolly Doodle all the day.

(*Chorus*) Fare thee well! . . . . . .

Oh, I came to a river and I couldn't get across,
Singing Polly Wolly Doodle all the day.
And I jumped upon a nigger, for I thought he was a hoss!
Singing Polly Wolly Doodle all the day.

(*Chorus*) Fare thee well! . . . . . .

Oh, a grasshopper sitting on a railroad track,
Singing Polly Wolly Doodle all the day.
A pickin' his teef with a carpet tack,
Singing Polly Wolly Doodle all the day.

(*Chorus*) Fare thee well! . . . . . .

Behind de barn down on my knees,
Singing Polly Wolly Doodle all the day.
I thought I heard a chicken sneeze,
Singing Polly Wolly Doodle all the day.

(*Chorus*) Fare thee well! . . . . . .

He sneezed so hard wid de whoopin' cough,
Singing Polly Wolly Doodle all the day.
He sneezed his head an' his tail right off,
Singing Polly Wolly Doodle all the day.

(*Chorus*) Fare thee well! . . . . . .

THERE IS A TAVERN IN THE TOWN

There is a tavern in the town, in the town,
And there my true love sits him down, sits him down,
And drinks his wine 'mid laughter free,
And never, never thinks of me.

(*Chorus*) Fare thee well, for I must leave thee,
Do not let the parting grieve thee,
But remember that the best of friends must part, must part.
Adieu, adieu, kind friends, adieu, adieu, adieu,
I can no longer stay with you, stay with you,
I'll hang my harp on a weeping willow tree,
And may the world go well with thee.

He left me for a damsel dark, damsel dark,
Each Friday night they used to spark, used to spark,
And now my love, once true to me,
Takes that dark damsel on his knee.

(*Chorus*) Fare thee well . . . . . .

Oh, dig my grave both wide and deep, wide and deep,
Put tombstones at my head and feet, head and feet,
And on my breast carve a turtle dove,
To signify I died of love.

(*Chorus*) Fare thee well . . . . . .

MY GRANDFATHER'S CLOCK

My grandfather's clock was too large for the shelf
So it stood ninety years on the floor;
It was taller by half than the old man himself,
Though it weighed not a penny-weight more.
It was bought on the morn of the day that he was born,
And was always his treasure and pride;
But it stopped, short, never to go again
When the old man died.

(*Chorus*) Ninety years without slumbering, tick, tock, tick, tock
His life's seconds numbering, tick, tock, tick, tock,
It stopped short—never to go again
When the old man died.

In watching its pendulum swing to and fro,
Many hours had he spent while a boy;
And in childhood and manhood the clock seem'd to know
And to share both his grief and his joy.
For it struck twenty-four when he enter'd at the door,
With a blooming and beautiful bride;
But it stopped, short, never to go again
When the old man died.

(*Chorus*) Ninety years without slumbering . . . . . .

My grandfather said, that of those he could hire
Not a servant so faithful he found;
For it wasted no time, and had but one desire—
At the close of each week to be wound.
And it kept in its place, not a frown upon its face,
And its hands never hung by its sides;
But it stopped, short, never to go again
When the old man died.

(*Chorus*) Ninety years without slumbering . . . . . .

It rang an alarm in the dead of the night,
An alarm that for years had been dumb;
And we knew that his spirit was pluming for flight
That his hour of departure had come.
Still the clock kept the time, with a soft and muffled chime
As we silently stood by his side;
But it stopped, short, never to go again
When the old man died.

(*Chorus*) Ninety years without slumbering . . . . . .

MEN OF HARLECH

Fierce the beacon light is flaming,
With its tongues of fire proclaiming
"Chieftains, sundered to your shaming,
Strongly now unite!"
At the call all Arfon rallies,
War-cries rend her hills and valleys,
Troop on troop, with headlong sallies,
Hurtle to the fight.
Chiefs lie dead and wounded,
Yet, where first 'twas grounded,
Freedom's flag still holds the crag.
Her trumpet still is sounded
There we'll keep her banner flying;
While the pale lips of the dying
Echo to our shout defying
"Harlech for the right!"

Shall the Saxon army shake you
Smite, pursue and overtake you?
Men of Harlech, God shall make you
Victors, blow for blow!
As the rivers of Ery
Sweep the vale with flooded fury,
Gwalia from her mountain eyrie
Thunders on the foe!
Now, avenging Briton,
Smite as he has smitten!
Let your rage on history's page
In Saxon blood be written!
His lance is long, but yours is longer,
Strong his sword, but yours is stronger!
One stroke more! and then your wronger
At your feet lies low!

LOCH LOMOND

By yon bonnie banks, and by yon bonnie braes,
Where the sun shines bright on Loch Lomond,
Where me and my true love were ever wont to gae,
On the bonnie, bonnie banks o' Loch Lomond.

(*Chorus*) Oh! ye'll tak' the high road and I'll tak' the low road,
And I'll be in Scotland afore ye:
But me and my true love will never meet again,
On the bonnie, bonnie banks o' Loch Lomond.

'Twas there that we parted, in yon shady glen,
On the steep, steep side o' Ben Lomond,
Where, in purple hue, the Hielan' hills we view,
And the moon comin' out in the gloamin'.

(*Chorus*) Oh! ye'll tak' the high road . . . . . .

The wee birdies sing and the wild flowers spring,
And in sunshine the waters are sleepin';
But the broken heart will ken nae second spring again,
Tho' the waefu' may cease frae their greetin'.

(*Chorus*) Oh! ye'll tak' the high road . . . . . .

LITTLE BROWN JUG

My wife and I liv'd all alone,
In a little log-hut we call'd our own;
She lov'd gin and I lov'd rum,
I tell you what, we'd lots of fun.

(*Chorus*) Ha, ha, ha, you and me,
"Little Brown Jug" don't I love thee.
Ha, ha, ha, you and me,
"Little Brown Jug" don't I love thee.

When I go toiling to my farm,
I take little "Brown Jug" under my arm;
I place it under a shady tree—
Little "Brown Jug", 'tis you and me.

(*Chorus*) Ha, ha, ha . . . . . .

If I'd a cow that gave such milk
I'd clothe her in the finest silk;
I'd feed her on the choicest hay,
And milk her forty times a day.

(*Chorus*) Ha, ha, ha . . . . . .

The rose is red, my nose is too,
The violet's blue, and so are you;
And yet I guess before I stop,
We'd better take another drop.

(*Chorus*) Ha, ha, ha . . . . . .

LAND OF THE SILVER BIRCH

Land of the silver birch, home of the beaver,
Where still the mighty moose wanders at will,
Blue lake and rocky shore, I will return once more.

(*Chorus*) Boom did-di-eye-di,
Boom did-di-eye-di,
Boom did-di-eye-di Boom.

My heart is sick for you here in the lowlands,
I will return to you, hills of the North.
Blue lake and rocky shore, I will return once more.

(*Chorus*) Boom . . . . . .

Swift as a silvèr fish, canoe of birch bark,
Thy mighty waterways carry me forth.
Blue lake and rocky shore, I will return once more.

(*Chorus*) Boom . . . . . .

There, where the blue lake lies I'll set my wigwam,
Close to the water's edge, silent and still.
Blue lake and rocky shore, I will return once more.

(*Chorus*) Boom . . . . . .

HERE'S A HEALTH UNTO HER MAJESTY

Here's a health unto Her Majesty
With a fa la la la la la la:
Confusion to her enemies
With a fa la la la la la la:
And he that will not drink her health,
We wish him neither wit nor wealth,
Nor yet a rope to hang himself,
With a fa la la la la la la la la,
With a fa la la la la la la.

THE GREAT AMERICAN RAILWAY

In eighteen hundred and sixty-one
The American railway was begun,
The American railway was begun,
The great American railway.

(*Chorus*) Patsy - atsy - or - ee - ay,
Patsy - atsy - or - ee - ay,
Patsy - atsy - or - ee - ay,
The great American railway.

In eighteen hundred and sixty-two
I found myself with nothing to do,
I found myself with nothing to do
Beside the American railway.

(*Chorus*) Patsy . . . . . .

In eighteen hundred and sixty-three
The overseer accepted me,
The overseer accepted me,
For work on the American railway.

(*Chorus*) Patsy . . . . . .

In eighteen hundred and sixty-four
My hands were tired and my feet were sore,
My hands were tired and my feet were sore,
From working on the Railway.

(*Chorus*) Patsy . . . . . .

In eighteen hundred and sixty-five
I found myself more dead than alive,
I found myself more dead than alive,
From work on the American railway.

(*Chorus*) Patsy . . . . . .

In eighteen hundred and sixty-six
I happened to tread on some dynamite sticks,
I happened to tread on some dynamite sticks,
While working on the railway.

(*Chorus*) Patsy . . . . . .

In eighteen hundred and sixty-seven
I found myself halfway to heaven,
I found myself halfway to heaven,
Above the American railway.

(*Chorus*) Patsy . . . . . .

In eighteen hundred and sixty-eight
I found my way through the Golden Gate,
I found my way through the Golden Gate
Above the American railway.

(*Chorus*) Patsy . . . . . .

In eighteen hundred and sixty-nine
A Cherub's harp and wings were mine,
A Cherub's harp and wings were mine
Above the American railway.

(*Chorus*) Patsy . . . . . .

In eighteen hundred and sixty-ten
If you want any more you can sing it again,
If you want any more you can sing it again
Above the American railway.

(*Chorus*) Patsy . . . . . .

EARLY ONE MORNING

Early one morning, just as the sun was rising,
I heard a maid sing in the valley below.

(*Chorus*) "Oh don't deceive me, O never leave me!
How could you use a poor maiden so?"

Remember the vows that you made to your Mary,
Remember the bow'r where you vowed to be true.

(*Chorus*) "Oh don't deceive me . . . . . ."

O gay is the garland, and fresh are the roses,
I've culled from the garden to bind on thy brow.

(*Chorus*) "Oh don't deceive me . . . . . ."

Thus sang the poor maiden, her sorrow bewailing,
Thus sang the poor maid in the valley below.

(*Chorus*) "Oh don't deceive me . . . . . ."

DRINK TO ME ONLY

Drink to me only with thine eyes,
And I will pledge with mine,
Or leave a kiss within the cup,
And I'll not look for wine.
The thirst that from the soul doth rise
Doth ask a drink divine,
But might I of Love's nectar sip,
I would not change for thine.

I sent thee late a rosy wreath,
Not so much hon'ring thee,
As giving it a hope that there
It could not wither'd be:
But thou thereon didst only breathe,
And sent'st it back to me
Since when it grows, and smells, I swear
Not of itself, but thee.

COME, LANDLORD, FILL THE FLOWING BOWL

Come, landlord, fill the flowing bowl,
Until it doth run over.
Come, landlord, fill the flowing bowl,
Until it doth run over.

(*Chorus*) For to-night we'll merry, merry be,
For to-night we'll merry, merry be,
For to-night we'll merry, merry be,
Tomorrow we'll be sober.

The man who drinketh small beer,
And goes to bed quite sober.
Fades as the leaves do fade,
That drop off in October.

(*Chorus*) For to-night we'll merry, merry be . . . . .

The man who drinketh strong beer
And goes to bed right mellow
Lives as he ought to live
And dies a jolly good fellow.

(*Chorus*) For to-night we'll merry, merry be . . . . .

But he who drinks just what he likes
And getteth half-seas over,
Lives until he dies (perhaps)
And then lies down in clover.

(*Chorus*) For to-night we'll merry, merry be . . . . .

The man who kisses a pretty girl
And goes and tells his mother,
Ought to have his lips cut off
And never kiss another.

(*Chorus*) For to-night we'll merry, merry be . . . . .

BOBBY SHAFTOE

(*Chorus*) Bobby Shaftoe's gone to sea,
Silver buckles on his knee;
He'll come back and marry me,
Bonny Bobby Shaftoe.

(*Solo*) Bobby Shaftoe's bright and fair,
Combing down his yellow hair,
He's my ain for ever-mair,
Bonny Bobby Shaftoe.

Bobby Shaftoe's tall and slim
He's always dressed so neat and trim
The lassies they all keek at him,
Bonny Bobby Shaftoe.

Bobby Shaftoe's gett'n a bairn
For to dangle on his airm,
On his airm and on his knee,
Bonny Bobby Shaftoe.

(*Last Chorus*) Bobby Shaftoe's been to sea
Silver buckles on his knee;
He's come back and married me,
Bonny Bobby Shaftoe.

BACK TO GILWELL

I used to be a Cuckoo, and a good old Cuckoo too,
But now I've finished cuckoo-ing, I don't know what to do,
I'm growing old and feeble and I can 'cuck' no more
So I'm going to work my ticket if I can.

(*Chorus*) Back to Gilwell, happy land,
I'm going to work my ticket if I can.

I used to be a 'Pecker, and a good old 'Pecker too,
But now I've finished 'pecking, I don't know what to do,
I'm growing old and feeble and I can 'peck' no more
So I'm going to work my ticket if I can.

(*Chorus*) Back to Gilwell . . . . . .

I used to be a Pigeon, and a good old Pigeon too,
But now I've finished pigeoning, I don't know what to do,
I'm growing old and feeble and I can 'pige' no more
So I'm going to work my ticket if I can.

(*Chorus*) Back to Gilwell . . . . . .

I used to be a Raven, and a good old Raven too,
But now I've finished ravening, I don't know what to do,
I'm growing old and feeble and I can 'rave' no more
So I'm going to work my ticket if I can.

(*Chorus*) Back to Gilwell . . . . . .

THE ASH GROVE

The Ash Grove how graceful, how plainly 'tis speaking,
The wind thro' it playing has language for me;
When over its branches the sunlight is breaking
A host of kind faces is gazing on me.
The friends of my childhood again are before me,
Fond memories waken as freely I roam,
With soft whispers laden its leaves rustle o'er me,
The Ash Grove, the Ash Grove that shelter'd my home.

My laughter is over, my step loses lightness,
Old countryside measures steel soft on my ear;
I only remember the past and its brightness,
The dear ones I mourn for again gather here.
From out of the shadows their loving looks greet me,
And wistfully searching the leafy green dome,
I find other faces fond bending to greet me;
The Ash Grove, the Ash Grove alone is my home!

JOHNNY HAD SOME MARMALADE

(*Tune:* John Brown's Body — roughly)

Johnny had some marmalade, and Johnny had some jam,
Johnny had some oyster sauce, and Johnny had some ham,
Johnny had some lemonade and then some ginger beer,
And Johnny wondered what it was that made him feel so queer.
Whoops went the marmalade and whoops went the jam,
Whoops went the oyster sauce and whoops went the ham,
Whoops went the lemonade and whoops the ginger beer,
And Johnny knew just what it was that made him feel so queer.

THE CUCKOO SONG

In the springtime sing this roundelay
As I travel along,
And I hear the blithe cuckoo
A-singing his song.

(*Chorus*) Hal–de–a . . . . . .
Haldea holay, O haldea cuckoo,
Haldea holay, O haldea cuckoo,
Haldea holay, O haldea cuckoo,
Haldea holay, Oho-o-o.

(NOTE: *Repeat with 2, 3, ... cuckoos*)

GREEN GROW THE RUSHES-OH (2 parts)

I'll sing you one-oh!
Green grow the rushes-oh!
What is your one-oh?
One is one and all alone and evermore shall be so.

I'll sing you two-oh!
Green grow the rushes-oh!
What are your two-oh?
Two, two the lily-white boys, clothe them all in green hi-ho.
One is one and all alone and evermore shall be so.

Three, three the rivals.

Four for the Gospel makers.

Five for the symbols at your door.

Six for the six proud walkers.

Seven for the seven stars in the sky.

Eight for the April rainers.

Nine for the nine bright shiners.

Ten for the ten commandments.

Eleven for the eleven that went to heaven.

Twelve for the twelve Apostles.

YOU'LL NEVER GO TO HEAVEN

A preacher went down in a cellar to pray,
And he prayed all night, and he prayed all day,
Oh a preacher went down in a cellar to pray,
And he prayed all night, and he prayed all day,
I ain't gonna grieve, my Lord, no more.

(*Chorus*) I ain't gonna grieve, my Lord, no more,
I ain't gonna grieve, my Lord, no more,
I ain't gonna grieve, my Lord, no more.

Oh you'll never go to Heaven, Oh you'll never go to Heaven,
In a limousine, in a limousine,
'Cause de Lord don't sell, 'cause de Lord don't sell,
No gasoline, no gasoline.
Oh you'll never go to Heaven in a limousine
'Cause de Lord don't sell no gasoline,
I ain't gonna grieve, my Lord, no more.

(*Chorus*) I ain't gonna grieve . . . . . .

Oh you'll never go to Heaven in a rocking chair,
'Cause de Lord don't like no lazybones there.

Oh you'll never go to Heaven in a woman's arms,
'Cause de Lord don't like those feminine charms.

Oh you'll never go to Heaven in a rowing boat,
'Cause a rowing boat won't keep afloat.

If you get there before I do
Just dig a hole and pull me through.

This is the end, there ain't no more,
St. Peter said as he locked the door.

(*There are numerous other verses you may add*)

THE WORM

(*Tune:* There's a long trail)

There's a long, long worm a crawling
    Across the flap of my tent,
I can hear the bugle calling
    And it's time that I went;
There's some icy water waiting
For me to take my morning dip,
    And when I return, I find that worm
    Is on my pillowslip.

That worm it went on crawling
    Throughout the heat of the day,
Round and round my tentpole,
    And it would not go away:
Oh! it really was a nuisance,
Because it spoilt my evening wash,
    And when I laid me down to rest
    That worm it went SQUISH - SQUASH!

WOOD SMOKE

(*Tune:* Waltzing Matilda)

Woodsmoke curling upwards, night shadows falling,
Troop gather round by the campfire's flame:
And our voices shall drown the night-bird's calling,
Singing the glory of our great game.
    Yell to the far skies your pet patrol cries,
    Tunefully chant in the birch-log's glow
    Tunes that are evergreen, rounds that have often been
    Sung by our brothers of long, long ago.

Softly sighs the night breeze rustling through the near trees,
Pale rides the moon in a star-studded sky:
And the flames glisten on the circle of bare knees,
A memory to store for the sweet by and by.
    Yell to the far skies your pet patrol cries,
    Tunefully chant in the birch-logs' glow
    Shanties rollicking, Scout stunts frolicking,
    Camp's finest hour we ever shall know.

But when flame starts to flicker and ashes turn white,
And we've completed our final round:
For the joys of the day and the spirit of this happy night
Sing praises to our Maker with joyous sound.
    Yell to the far skies your pet patrol cries,
    Tunefully chant in the birch-logs' glow
    Tunes that are evergreen, rounds that have often been
    Sung by our brothers of long, long ago.

WAY DOWN SOUTH

(*Tune:* Old MacDougall)

Old MacDougall had a farm,
Way down yonder in the cornfields;
And on that farm he had some cows,
Way down yonder in the cornfields;
With a moo-moo here, moo-moo there,
Here a moo, there a moo, everywhere a moo-moo,
Old MacDougall had a farm,
Way down yonder in the cornfields.

(*Chorus*) O way down South, O way down South
Where the water melons grow, where the water melons grow,
Back to my home, back to my home,
I dare not go, I dare not go,
For if I do, for if I do,
My mother would say
What would she say?
"Have you ever seen a cow with a green eyebrow
Down in the old Red Lion?"

Old MacDougall had a farm,
Way down yonder in the cornfields;
And on that farm he had some sheep,
Way down yonder in the cornfields.
With a baa-baa here, baa-baa there,
Here a baa, there a baa, everywhere a baa-baa,
With a moo-moo here, moo-moo there,
Here a moo, there a moo, everywhere a moo-moo,
Old MacDougall had a farm,
Way down yonder in the cornfields.

(*Chorus*) O way down South . . . . . .

(*And so on with dogs, turkeys, pigs, terrier, etc.*)

DID YOU EVER SEE

(*Chorus*) Did you ever see,
Did you ever see,
Did you ever see,
Such a funny thing before?

Now I've got an Auntie Morgan
And she plays the chapel organ,
And she also rings the bell
When the people go to heaven:

(*Chorus*) Did you ever see . . . . . .

Now I've got a brother Jack,
For Cardiff he's full back,
They were playing at Llanelly,
Someone kicked him in the bethly:

(*Chorus*) Did you ever see . . . . . .

Now I've got a brother Mike
And he had a motor-bike,
But he sold it for a tanner
For he hadn't got a spanner:

(*Chorus*) Did you ever see . . . . . .

Now I've got a brother Sam
And he drives a 'lectric tram,
When the conductor rings the bell
The tram just goes like lightning.

(*Chorus*) Did you ever see . . . . . .

Now the pubs down in Wales
They all sell the finest ales;
If you want a drink on Sunday
Well, you'll have to wait till Monday:

(*Chorus*) Did you ever see . . . . . .

WALTZING MATILDA

Once a jolly swagman camped by a billabong,
Under the shade of a coolabah tree,
And he sang as he watched and waited till his billy boiled,
"You'll come a-Waltzing Matilda with me".

(*Chorus*) "Waltzing Matilda, Waltzing Matilda,
You'll come a-Waltzing Matilda with me"
And he sang as he watched and waited till his billy boiled,
"You'll come a-Waltzing Matilda with me".

Down came a jumbuck to drink at that billabong,
Up jumped the swagman and grabbed him with glee,
And he sang as he tucked that jumbuck in his tuckerbag,
"You'll come a-Waltzing Matilda with me".

(*Chorus*) "Waltzing Matilda . . . . . .

Up rode the squatter, mounted on his thoroughbred,
Down came the troopers, one, two, three:
"Where's that jolly jumbuck you've got in your tuckerbag?
You'll come a-Waltzing Matilda with me".

(*Chorus*) "Waltzing Matilda . . . . . .

Up jumped the swagman, jumped into that billabong,
"You'll never take me alive," said he,
And his ghost may be heard as you pass by that billabong,
"You'll come a-Waltzing Matilda with me".

(*Chorus*) Waltzing Matilda . . . . . .

THE TWELVE DAYS OF CHRISTMAS

On the first day of Christmas
My true love sent to me
    A partridge in a pear tree.

On the second day of Christmas
My true love sent to me
    Two turtle doves,
    And a partridge in a pear tree.

On the third day of Christmas
My true love sent to me
    Three French hens,
    Two turtle doves,
    And a partridge in a pear tree.

Fourth:	Four calling birds
Fifth:	Five gold rings
Sixth:	Six geese a-laying
Seventh:	Seven swans a-swimming
Eighth:	Eight maids a-milking
Ninth:	Nine ladies dancing
Tenth:	Ten Lords a-leaping
Eleventh:	Eleven pipers piping
Twelfth:	Twelve drummers drumming

THEY WERE ONLY PLAYING LEAPFROG

(*Tune:* John Brown's Body)

One grasshopper hopped across another grasshopper's back,
One grasshopper hopped across another grasshopper's back,
One grasshopper hopped across another grasshopper's back,
As they all went marching home.

(*Chorus*) They were only playing leapfrog,
They were only playing leapfrog,
They were only playing leapfrog,
And the smoke went up the chimney just the same.

A spider spied a spider on another spider's back,
(*Repeat three times*)

(*Chorus*) They were only playing leapfrog . . . . . .

One hedgehog edged up the hedge as another hedgehog edged down,
(*Repeat three times*)

(*Chorus*) They were only playing leapfrog . . . . . .

A busy buzzing bumble bee was busily buzzing by,
(*Repeat three times*)

(*Chorus*) They were only playing leapfrog . . . . . .

THAT'S THE WORST OF CAMP

(*Tune:* Coming thro' the Rye)

Oft a body hears a body
Say a muttered "Blow",
In the morning when the cock
Is singing soft and low.
Oh! that six-ack-emma feeling
When the grass is damp,
The fire is out, and you are cook—
But that's the worst of camp!
But that's the worst of camp!

Oft a body sees a body
Coming in with sticks;
Staggering slowly up the hill
With load enough for six.
Oh! that bent and aged feeling
Longing for a gamp
To help your tottering steps along—
But that's the worst of camp!

Oft a body sees a body
Rushing to and fro.
"Where's the map?" "There's no more Vim!"
"It's going to rain, I know!"
Oh! that unabated feeling
When you long to stamp
And rave and throw the plates about—
But that's the worst of camp!

At last a body sees a body
Striking camp to go,
Take down tents and pack them up
With sorrow, rage and woe.
Oh! that dull and hopeless feeling
As you homeward tramp:
You'd give your gum boots to be back—
But that's the worst of camp!

TEN BLUEBOTTLES
(*Tune:* Ten Green Bottles)

Ten Bluebottles sitting on the meat,
Ten Bluebottles sitting on the meat,
And if one Bluebottle
Should wipe its dirty feet—
Then somebody's dinner
Would not be fit to eat.

Nine Bluebottles, eight, seven, etc.

THE SWEETEST GIRL

(*Tune:* John Peel)

The sweetest girl I ever met
Was sucking up acid in a glass pipette
I said to her, "I've never yet
Tried sucking up acid in a pip-pipette."

For the sight of that maid had gone to my head,
And I cared not a jot what I did or said
I shall love that fair maid till of love I am dead,
For she captured my heart in the morning.

Said she to me, "Why then, you'd better share
With me this here pipette."
So two by two our four lips met
A-sucking nitric acid in a pip-pipette.

And then I thought "I dare not let my class
See me share this pipette."
So I withdrew my lips unwet
And left her to the acid in the pip-pipette.

The stuff was concentrated, yet
She sucked away at that pipette,
And so I lost my darling pet
Through letting her suck acid in a pip-pipette.

THE PAW-PAW PATCH

(*Tune:* Michael Finnigan)

That is where I met my Susie,
That is where I met my Susie,
That is where I met my Susie,
Way down yonder in the paw-paw patch.

(*Chorus*) Picking up paw-paws, putting them in the basket,
Picking up paw-paws, putting them in the basket,
Picking up paw-paws, putting them in the basket,
Way down yonder in the paw-paw patch.

That is where I cuddled and kissed her,
That is where I cuddled and kissed her,
That is where I cuddled and kissed her,
Way down yonder in the paw-paw patch.

(*Chorus*) Picking up paw-paws . . . . . .

That is where I married my Susie . . . . . .

That is where we raised our family . . . . . .

That is where I buried my Susie . . . . . .

OUR FAMILY

(*Tune:* My Bonny)

My father makes counterfeit money,
My mother brews synthetic gin,
My sister sells kisses to sailors—
By jove, how the money rolls in!

(*Chorus*) Rolls in, rolls in, by jove how the money rolls in, rolls in
Rolls in, rolls in, by jove how the money rolls in!

My brother's a slum missionary,
Saving young maidens from sin,
He'll save you a blonde for a shilling—
By jove, how the money rolls in!

(*Chorus*) Rolls in, rolls in . . . . . .

My aunt keeps a girls' seminary,
Teaching young girls to begin,
She doesn't say where they're to finish—
By jove, how the money rolls in!

(*Chorus*) Rolls in, rolls in . . . . . .

NATIONAL ANTHEM OF THE ANCIENT BRITONS

(*Tune:* Men of Harlech)

What's the good of wearing braces, vests and pants and boots with laces,
Spats, or hats you buy in places down in Brompton Road?
What's the use of shirts of cotton, studs that always get forgotten?
These affairs are simply rotten: better far is woad.
Woad's the stuff to show, men;
Woad to scare your foe, men.
Boil it to a brilliant hue
And rub it on your back and your abdomen.
Ancient Briton never hit on
Anything as good as woad to fit on:
Neck, or knees, or where you sit on—
Tailors, you be blowed!

Romans came across the Channel all wrapped up in tin and flannel;
Half a pint of woad per man'll dress us more than these.
Saxons, you can waste your stitches building beds for bugs in breeches;
We have woad to clothe us, which is not a nest for fleas.
Roman, keep your armours;
Saxon, your pyjamas—
Hairy coats were meant for goats,
Gorillas, yaks, retriever dogs and llamas.
Tramp up Snowdon with your woad on,
Never mind if we get rained or blowed on,
Never want a button sewed on—
Go it, Ancient B's!

MY GAL'S A CORKER

My Gal's a corker, she's a New Yorker,
I buy her everything to keep her in clothes;
She's got a head of hair
Just like a grizzly bear—
That's where all my money goes!

(*Chorus*) Oompery, oompery, oom-pom-pom
Oompery, oompery, oom-pom-pom.

My Gal's a corker, she's a New Yorker,
I buy her everything to keep her in clothes;
She's got a pair of eyes
Just like two custard pies—
That's where all my money goes!

(*Chorus*) Oompery, oompery . . . . . .

My Gal's a corker, she's a New Yorker,
I buy her everything to keep her in clothes;
She's got a pair of hips
Just like two battleships—
That's where all my money goes!

(*Chorus*) Oompery, oompery . . . . . .

My Gal's a corker, she's a New Yorker,
I buy her everything to keep her in clothes;
She's got a pair of legs
Just like two brandy kegs—
That's where all my money goes!

(*Chorus*) Oompery, oompery . . . . . .

My Gal's a corker, she's a New Yorker,
I buy her everything to keep her in clothes;
She's got a pair of feet
Just like two plates of meat—
That's where all my money goes!

(*Chorus*) Oompery, oompery . . . . . .

LAST ROUND-UP

I'm heading for the last round-up,
Diddle de de, de dah, de dah,
Going to saddle Old Paint for the last time and ri . . . de.
So long old pal, it's time your tears were fall . . . ing,
I'm heading for the last round up.
Get along little Dogey, get along little Dogey,
Get along little Dogey, get along.

Get along little Dogey, get along little Dogey,
Get along little Dogey, get along.
I'm heading for the last round-up,
Diddle de de, de dah, de dah,
To the far away ranch of the Boss in the sky . . . y,
Where they catch the strays and brand them, there go I . . . I.
I'm heading for the last round-up,
Get along little Dogey, get along little Dogey,
Get along little Dogey, get along.

KAFOOZALUM

In ancient days within the east
There lived a Turk, a horrid beast,
Who did the prophet's holy work
As Baba of Jerusalem.
He had a daughter sweet and smirk,
Complexion fair and dark blue hair,
And nought about her like a Turk
Except the name, Kafoozalum.

(*Chorus*) Hi, Hi, Kafoozalum, Kafoozalum, Kafoozalum,
Hi, Hi, Kafoozalum, daughter of the Baba.

A youth resided near to she:
A perfect lamb, his name was Sam.
He came of ancient pedigree,
He came from old Methusalem.
He drove a trade that prospered well
In skins of cats and ancient hats,
And, ringing at the front door bell,
He saw and loved Kafoozalum.

(*Chorus*) Hi, Hi, Kafoozalum . . . . . .

If Sam had been a Mussulman
He might have sold the Baba Old,
And with a verse of Al Koran
He managed to bamboozle 'im.
But, oh dear no! He tried a scheme:
Passed one night late the area gate,
And hurried to the Turk's harem
To carry off Kafoozalum.

(*Chorus*) Hi, Hi, Kafoozalum . . . . . .

The Baba was about to smoke;
His slaves rushed in with horrid din,
"Ashala, dogs thy house have broke;
Come down, my Lord, and toozle 'em."
The Baba wreathed his face in smiles,
Came down the stair and witnessed there
A gentleman in three old tiles
A-kissing of Kafoozalum.

(*Chorus*) Hi, Hi, Kafoozalum . . . . .

The pious Baba said no more
Than twenty prayers, then went upstairs
And took a bow string from the drawer,
And came down to Kafoozalum.
The maiden and the youth he took
And choked them both and, nothing loth,
He pitched them both into the brook
Of Kedron, by Jerusalem.

(*Chorus*) Hi, Hi, Kafoozalum . . . . .

HE SAT ON THE VERANDA

He sat on the veranda and smoked his cigar,
Smoked his cigar, smoked his cigar,
He sat on the veranda and smoked his cigar,
Smoked his cigar-ha-ha-ha.

She sat down beside him and oh how she sighed,
Oh how she sighed, oh how she sighed,
She sat down beside him and oh how she sighed,
Oh how she sigh-hi-hi-highed.

He said, "How I love you," but oh how he lied,
Oh how he lied, oh how he lied,
He said, "How I love you," but oh how he lied,
Oh how he lie-hi-hi-hied.

Then they got married and somehow she died,
Somehow she died, somehow she died,
She was took ill, and somehow she died,
Somehow she die-hi-hi-hied.

He went to the funeral but just for the ride,
Just for the ride, just for the ride,
He went to the funeral but just for the ride,
Just for the ri-hi-hi-hide.

He sat on her tombstone and laughed till he died,
Laughed till he died, laughed till he died,
He sat on her tombstone, and laughed till he died,
Laughed till he die-hi-hi-hied.

She went to Heaven and flip-flap she flies,
Flip-flap she flies, flip-flap she flies,
She went to Heaven and flip-flap she flies,
Flip-flap she fly-hi-hi-hies.

He went to the other place and frizzles and fries,
Frizzles and fries, frizzles and fries,
He went to the other place and frizzles and fries,
Frizzles and fry-hi-hi-hies.

The moral of this story is never tell a lie,
    Never tell a lie, never tell a lie,
Because if you do you will frizzle and fry,
    Frizzle and fry-hi-hi-hi-hy.

GHOST'S TALE

Have you ever thought as the hearse goes by
That some day you will surely die?
(*Chorus*) Ooo-oo-ooh, aaa-aa-aah,
Happy we shall be!

The sexton will come and toll his bell
The people will gather and laugh like—
(*Chorus*) Ooo-oo-ooh . . . . . .

They'll wrap you up in a wooden shirt,
And cover you with lumps of dirt.
(*Chorus*) Ooo-oo-ooh . . . . . .

The worms crawl in and the worms crawl out,
They crawl in thin—and they crawl out stout.
(*Chorus*) Ooo-oo-ooh . . . . . .

Your cheeks fall in and your eyes fall out,
Your brain comes trickling down your snout.
(*Chorus*) Ooo-oo-ooh . . . . . .

Your hair comes out, and you lose your nose,
The nails fall out of your fingers and toes.
(*Chorus*) Ooo-oo-ooh . . . . . .

Your blood dries up and your skin goes green,
Such a lovely sight you've rarely seen.
(*Chorus*) Ooo-oo-ooh . . . . . .

The maggots grow fat and the weeds grow firm,
But cows eat grass and birds eat worms.
(*Chorus*) Ooo-oo-ooh . . . . . .

Now men eat cows and men eat birds,
And egg makes cake, and milk makes curds.
(*Chorus*) Ooo-oo-ooh . . . . . .

Then up to heaven you'll surely go,
They won't let you in—they've seen you before.
(*Chorus*) Ooo-oo-ooh . . . . . .

Then down to hell, the devil will grin;
He'll say, "Come inside, there are plenty within—
to keep the home fires burning."
(*Chorus*) Ooo-oo-ooh . . . . . .

FIRE DOWN BELOW

Fire in the galley, fire down below,
It's fetch a bucket of water, boys, there's fire down below.

(*Chorus*) Fire, fire, fire down below,
It's fetch a bucket of water, boys,
There's fire down below.

Fire in the forepeak, fire down below,
It's fetch a bucket of water, boys, there's fire down below.

(*Chorus*) Fire, fire . . . . . .

Fire in the windlass, fire in the chain,
It's fetch a bucket of water, girls, and put it out again.

(*Chorus*) Fire, fire . . . . . .

EMBROCATION

(*Tune:* Cockles and Mussels)

There was an old fellow
Who never felt well—oh,
And always complained of an ailment or two;
But he drank embrocation
To gain inspiration,
And now he's as fit as a young kangaroo.

(*Chorus*) Drink em-embrocation,
To gain inspiration,
And you'll be as fit as a young kangaroo.

Alone in his sorrow,
He never could borrow;
He hadn't a friend, but whene'er he felt blue
He drank embrocation
And found consolation,
And he was as hearty as flies at the zoo.

(*Chorus*) Drink em-embrocation,
And find consolation,
And you'll be as hearty as flies at the zoo.

From a gate in a meadow
He fell on his head—oh,
And kicked all his teeth out and swallowed them too,
But he drank embrocation
Without hesitation,
And now he can bite like a woolamaloo.

(*Chorus*) Drink em-embrocation,
Without hesitation,
And then you will bite like a woolamaloo.

So instead of tobacco
When things all look black-oh,
Just take my advice—that's all you have to do,
Is to drink embrocation
Whatever your station,
And you'll be as happy as Winnie the Pooh.

(*Chorus*) Whatever your station
Drink em-embrocation,
And you'll be as happy as Winnie the Pooh.

DARKY SUNDAY SCHOOL

(*Chorus*) Old folks, young folks, everybody come,
Join the Darky Sunday School and make yourself at home,
Bring a stick of chewing gum and sit upon the floor,
And we'll tell you Bible stories that you've never heard before.

Adam was the first man, at least we do believe,
Went into the garden and was introduced to Eve,
What it was they did there we really cannot say,
But that is the reason why we're gathered here today.

(*Chorus*) Old folks . . . . . .

Jonah was a traveller, so says the ancient tale,
He booked a steerage passage on a transatlantic whale
The atmospheric pressure got heavy on his chest,
So he simply pressed the button and the whale did the rest.

(*Chorus*) Old folks . . . . . .

Pharaoh had a daughter with a most bewitching smile,
She found the infant Moses by the waters of the Nile,
She took the child to father and Pharaoh he turned pale,
"It's just about as likely as Jonah and the whale."

(*Chorus*) Old folks . . . . . .

Shadrack, Meshack and Abednego,
Annoyed the King of Egypt, in the fire they had to go,
Into the fiery furnace to burn away the chaff,
But they wore asbestos undies and gave the King a laugh.

(*Chorus*) Old folks . . . . . .

Cain he was a bad man and Abel he was good,
Cain caned his brother like any brother would,
Abel didn't like it so he asked him to refrain,
But Cain wasn't able, so Abel got the cane.

(*Chorus*) Old folks . . . . . .

Goliath was a hefty man, a mighty man was he,
While David was a little man about as big as me.
David took a little sling and half a brick as well,
When David slung the brick at him, Goliath went to—

(*Chorus*) Old folks . . . . . .

Ruth she was a flapper of a very modern type,
She wore short skirts and rode a motor-bike,
She used that wicked lip-stick and her eye was of the glad,
But the Salvation Army saved her from the bad.

(*Chorus*) Old folks . . . . . .

Now our little Sunday School is finished for the day,
I hope you're feeling better in every kind of way,
I feel it sounds much better if we do it all in verse,
On Monday next at half past seven the choir will rehearse.

(*Chorus*) Old folks . . . . . .

COOK IS A GEM

(*Tune:* My Bonny)

We've had lots of songs about camping,
The joys of the trek and the trail,
We've known of the glories of sing-songs,
Adventures with tents in a gale:
But what makes a man's outdoor living
Is not the camp-site or the brook,
'Tis just one chap—prince of good fellows,
That treasure of Scouters—the Cook!

He knows all there is about campfires
He knows just how porridge should be,
He cooks to a turn all the bacon,
Provides ripping coffee and tea.
At stews and e'en roasts he is handy,
His flapjacks and puddings a treat;
He's great on potatoes of all kinds,
His bully beef meals hard to beat.

He'll get you a meal in a hurry,
In temper he's almost a saint;
With soup he's just a magician,
You think that it's something it ain't!
What would outdoor life be without him?
He ought to have medals of gold,
So here's to the king of the camp fire,
Our cook—may he never grow old.

CAMP-FIRE LILLI MARLENE

With the scent of woodsmoke drifting in the air,
In the glow of firelight we always love to share,
Visions of camp-fires all return,
And as the logs flare up and burn,
We dream of bygone camp-fires
And long for those to come.

As the night gets darker the flames begin to die,
Logs are piled on higher and sparks fly to the sky,
The stars above look kindly down,
Like sequins on a velvet gown,
The night is warm and peaceful
As we sing the songs we love.

So throughout the winter shall our thoughts return,
To that lovely campsite by the sparkling burn,
The work we did, the games we played,
The food we cooked, the fires we laid,
But above all, dear camp-fire,
We'll remember you.

Tongues of yellow fire flickering up on high,
Reaching twisting fingers up to a starlit sky,
Voices recall songs old and new,
Songs once dear to fathers, too,
Who dreamed of bygone camp-fires,
And longed for those to come.

Gently dying embers cast a rosy glow,
Voices slowly sinking to tones so soft and low,
Slowly, upon the still night air,
Fall faithful voices, hushed in prayer,
That dream of bygone camp-fires,
And long for those to come.

BLOW THE MAN DOWN

Come all you young fellows that follow the sea,
Way-hay, blow the man down,
And please pay attention and listen to me,
Give us some time to blow the man down.

On board the *Black Baller* I first served my time,
Way-hay, blow the man down,
And on the *Black Baller* I wasted my time,
Give us some time to blow the man down.

There were tinkers and tailors and sailors and all,
Way-hay, blow the man down,
That shipped for good seamen on board the *Black Ball*,
Give us some time to blow the man down.

'Tis larboard and starboard you jump to the call,
Way-hay, blow the man down,
When kicking Jack Williams commands the *Black Ball*,
Give us some time to blow the man down.

BITS OF HISTORY

(*Tune:* Darky Sunday School)

King Alfred cooked a damper on a lady's grate,
But his mind was occupied with affairs of state,
To eat that burnt up cinder I'm sure you would refuse,
So Alfred kept it till next morn to clean his patent shoes.

(*Chorus*) Old folk, young folk, everybody come
To our little village school and make yourselves at home,
Close the windows carefully and fasten up the door,
And we'll tell you bits of history you've never heard before.

The easiest date in history that in your memory sticks,
When William came from Normandy in one-o-double-six,
He met his old friend Harold down on Hastings pier
And stuck an arrow in his eye and gave him a thick ear.

(*Chorus*) Old folk . . . . . .

Richard Coeur de Lion was imprisoned by the duke,
Blondell, his pet minstrel, played outside on his uke;
He played King Richard's favourite tune "Oh he's my baby-face,"
And as he sang the treble part, King Richard sang the bass.

(*Chorus*) Old folk . . . . . .

Brave Sir Walter Raleigh brought tobacco from the West,
And laid his jacket in the mud to please his good Queen Bess,
Then she asked him when he next would sail the Seven Seas,
He said "Do have a Woodbine" and she answered "Players please".

(*Chorus*) Old folk . . . . . .

Good King Charlie lost his head in sixteen-forty-nine,
He wished the beak had given him the option of a fine,
When it was all over his neck was very sore,
So he did not do like Oliver and ask for any more.

(*Chorus*) Old folk . . . . . .

Anne Stuart Queen of England was, she did her level best,
Her twenty-four young infants were quickly laid to rest,
She worried lest her dynasty be left upon the shelf,
And now, kind friends, sad to relate, Queen Anne is dead herself.

(*Chorus*) Old folk . . . . . .

King Henry put an advert in asking for a wife,
For he'd cut the last one's head off with a carving knife.
When he had an interview, he turned round in alarm,
For Anne Boleyn had just come in, with 'er 'ead tucked underneath 'er arm.

(*Chorus*) Old folk . . . . . .

BIRDS IN THE WILDERNESS

My old massa he bought a horserum,
He bought a horserum,
He bought a horserum,
My old massa he bought a horserum,
Way down Alabama.

(*Chorus—in four parts*)
(*1st*) Here we sit like birds in the wilderness,
(*2nd*) Bees in the honey pot,
(*3rd*) Flies in the marmalade,
(*4th*) Here we sit like spuds in the billy can,
(*All*) Way down Alabama.

My old massa he got a kickerum . . . . . .
(*Chorus*) Here we sit . . . . . .

My old massa he fell a sickerum . . . . . .
(*Chorus*) Here we sit . . . . . .

My old massa sent for the doctorum . . . . . .
(*Chorus*) Here we sit . . . . . .

My old doctor couldn't effect a cureum . . . . . .
(*Chorus*) Here we sit . . . . . .

My old massa he fell a deaderum . . . . . .
(*Chorus*) Here we sit . . . . . .

YE BANKS AND BRAES

Ye banks and braes o' bonnie Doon,
How can ye bloom sae fresh and fair?
How can ye chaunt, ye little birds,
And I sae weary, fu' o' care?
Ye'll break my heart, ye warbling birds,
That warble on the flow'ry thorn,
Ye mind me o' departed joys,
Departed never to return.

Oft ha'e I roved by bonnie Doon,
By morning and by evening shine,
To hear the birds sing o' their loves,
As fondly once I sang o' mine;
Wi' lightsome heart I stretched my hand,
And pu'd a rose-bud from the tree
But my fause lover stole the rose
And left, and left the thorn wi' me.

WHAT SHALL WE DO WITH THE DRUNKEN SAILOR

What shall we do with the drunken sailor,
What shall we do with the drunken sailor,
What shall we do with the drunken sailor,
Early in the morning?

(*Chorus*) Hooray and up she rises,
Hooray and up she rises,
Hooray and up she rises,
Early in the morning.

Put him in the long-boat 'till he's sober.

Pull out the plug and wet him all over.

Put him in the scuppers with a hose-pipe on him.

Heave him by the leg in a running bowlin'.

Tie him on the taffrail when she's yard-arm under.

That's what we'll do with the drunken sailor.

CLEMENTINE

In a cavern, in a canyon,
Excavating for a mine,
Dwelt a miner, forty-niner,
And his daughter Clementine.

(*Chorus*) Oh my darling, oh my darling,
Oh my darling, Clementine!
Thou art lost and gone for ever;
Dreadful sorry, Clementine!

Light she was and like a fairy,
And her shoes were number nine;
Herring boxes without topses,
Sandals were for Clementine.

(*Chorus*) Oh my darling . . . . . .

Drove she duckling to the water
Every morning just at nine;
Hit her foot against a splinter,
Fell into the foaming brine.

(*Chorus*) Oh my darling . . . . . .

Saw her lips above the water,
Blowing bubbles, mighty fine;
But alas! I was no swimmer
So I lost my Clementine.

(*Chorus*) Oh my darling . . . . . .

How I missed her, how I missed her,
How I missed my Clementine!
But I kissed her little sister,
And forgot my Clementine.

(*Chorus*) Oh my darling . . . . . .

And the moral of this story
All you Scouts might well define:
Mouth-to-mouth resuscitation
Would have saved my Clementine.

(*Chorus*) Oh my darling . . . . .

PICK A BALE OF COTTON

Jump down, turn around, pick a bale of cotton,
Jump down, turn around, pick a bale a day.
Jump down, turn around, pick a bale of cotton,
Jump down, turn around, pick a bale a day.

O Lordy, pick a bale of cotton,
O Lordy, pick a bale a day.
O Lordy, pick a bale of cotton,
O Lordy, pick a bale a day.

Pick a pick a pick a pick a pick a bale of cotton,
Pick a pick a pick a pick a pick a bale a day.
Pick a pick a pick a pick a pick a bale of cotton,
Pick a pick a pick a pick a pick a bale a day.

O Lordy, pick a bale of cotton,
O Lordy, pick a bale a day.
O Lordy, pick a bale of cotton,
O Lordy, pick a bale a day.

Me and my wife, we picked a bale of cotton,
Me and my wife, we picked a bale a day.
Me and my wife, we picked a bale of cotton,
Me and my wife, we picked a bale a day.

O Lordy, pick a bale of cotton,
O Lordy, pick a bale a day.
O Lordy, pick a bale of cotton,
O Lordy, pick a bale a day.

AND THE GREEN GRASS GREW ALL ROUND

There was a tree upon a hill,
The finest tree you ever did see,
And the tree was on a hill,
And the hill stood still.

(*Chorus*) And the green grass grew all round my boys,
The green grass grew all round.
The green grass grew all round my boys,
And the green grass grew all round.

There was a branch upon that tree,
The finest branch you ever did see,
And the branch was on the tree,
And the tree was on the hill,
And the hill stood still.

There was a twig upon that branch, etc.

There was a leaf upon that twig, etc.

There was a nest upon that leaf, etc.

There was a bird upon that nest, etc.

There was a wing upon that bird, etc.

There was a feather upon that wing, etc.

There was a flea upon that feather,
The finest flea you ever did see,
And the flea was on the feather,
And the feather was on the wing,
And the wing was on the bird,
And the bird was on the nest,
And the nest was on the leaf,
And the leaf was on the twig,
And the twig was on the branch,

And the branch was on the tree,
And the tree was on the hill,
And the hill stood still.

(*Chorus*) And the green grass grew . . . . . .

ON TOP OF SPAGHETTI

(*Tune:* On Top of Old Smoky)

On top of spaghetti,
All covered in cheese,
I lost my poor meat ball
When somebody sneezed.

It rolled off the table
And onto the floor,
And then my poor meat ball
Rolled out of the door.

It rolled down the garden
And under a bush,
And then my poor meat ball
Was nothing but mush!

If you have spaghetti,
All covered in cheese,
Hold onto your meat ball,
'Cos someone might sneeze!

HEART OF OAK

Come, cheer up, my lads, 'tis to glory we steer,
To add something new to this wonderful year;
To honour we call you, not press you like slaves—
For who are so free as the sons of the waves?

(*Chorus*) Heart of oak are our ships,
Jolly tars are our men;
We always are ready;
Steady, boys, steady;
We'll fight and we'll conquer again and again.

We ne'er see our foes but we wish them to stay,
They never see us but they wish us away;
If they run, why, we follow, and run them ashore,
And if they won't fight us, we cannot do more.

(*Chorus*) Heart of oak . . . . . .

We'll still make them fear, and we'll still make them flee,
And drub 'em on shore as we've drubb'd 'em at sea;
Then cheer up, my lads, with one heart let us sing,
Our soldiers, our sailors, our statesmen, our King.

(*Chorus*) Heart of oak . . . . . .

MICHAEL FINNAGEN

There was an old man named Michael Finnagen,
He grew whiskers on his chinagen,
The wind came out and blew them in agen,
Poor old Michael Finnagen, begin agen.

There was an old man named Michael Finnagen,
He got drunk through drinking ginagen,
Thus he wasted all his tinagen,
Poor old Michael Finnagen, begin agen.

There was an old man named Michael Finnagen,
He kicked up an awful dinagen,
Because they said he must not sinagen,
Poor old Michael Finnagen, begin agen.

There was an old man named Michael Finnagen,
He went fishing with a pinagen.
Caught a fish but dropped it in agen,
Poor old Michael Finnagen, begin agen.

There was an old man named Michael Finnagen,
Climbed a tree and barked his shinagen,
Took off several yards of skinagen,
Poor old Michael Finnagen, begin agen.

There was an old man named Michael Finnagen,
He grew fat and then grew thin agen,
Then he died, and had to begin agen,
Poor old Michael Finnagen, begin agen.

SMILING ALONG

(*Tune:* John Brown's Body)

It's not a lot of bother just to S-M-I-L-E,
It's not a lot of bother just to S-M-I-L-E,
It's not a lot of bother just to S-M-I-L-E,
If you'll only be like me and S-M-I-L-E.

It's not a lot of bother just to G-R-I-N grin
. . . .

It's not a lot of bother just to S-I-N-G sing
. . . .

It's not a lot of bother just to J-E-S-T jest
. . . .

It's not a lot of bother just to L-A-U-G-H
. . . .

OLD SMOKY

On top of Old Smoky, all covered with snow,
I lost my true lover, from a-courtin' to slow.

On top of Old Smoky, I went there to weep,
Cause a false-hearted lover, is worse than a thief.

For a thief he will rob you, and take what you have
But a false-hearted lover, will send you to your grave.

She'll hug you and kiss you, and tell you more lies
Than the cross-ties on a railroad, and stars in the skies.

Come all you fair maidens, take warning from me
Don't place your affections in a green willow tree.

For the roots they will wither, and the leaves they will die
And you'll soon be forgotten, and never know why.

On top of Old Smoky, all covered with snow
I lost my true lover, from a-courtin' too slow.

SHORT SONGS AND ROUNDS

PUNCHINELLO

Oh dear Mother, I'm to be married to Mister Punchinello,
Oh dear Mother, I'm to be married to Mister Punchinello,
To Mister Punch — to Mister Chin — to Mister Ell — to
Mister O, Punch-in-el-lo.

EEN GONYÂMA

Een gonyâma,
Gonyâma, invooboo.
Yay bôh, yah bôh
Invoo-boo.

I'M A LITTLE TEAPOT

(*Tune:* Underneath the spreading chestnut tree)

I'm a little teapot, short and stout,
Here's my handle, here's my spout;
When the water's boiling hear me shout,
"Fill me up and pour me out!"

BLACK CROW'S SPIRIT

(*Tune:* John Brown's Body)

Black Crow's spirit's in his happy hunting ground,
Black Crow's spirit's in his happy hunting ground,
Black Crow's spirit's in his happy hunting ground,
Ever so far away.
Minne – minne – minne – ha – ha,
Hia – hia – hiawatha,
Minne – minne – minne – ha – ha,
Ever so far away.

WE'RE ON THE SCOUTING TRAIL (2-8 parts)

We're on the Scouting trail,
We're on the Scouting trail,
Singing, singing, everybody singing,
Scouting bound.

(NOTE: *The second part begins when the first part reaches the word 'trail'*).

ONE BOTTLE BEER (3 parts)

1st One bottle beer, two bottle beer, three bottle beer, four bottle beer,
Five bottle beer, six bottle beer, seven seven bottle beer.

2nd Oh, you can't put your muck in our dustbin, our dustbin, our dustbin,
You can't put your muck in our dustbin, our dustbin's full.

3rd Fish and chips and vinegar, vinegar, vinegar;
Fish and chips and vinegar, pepper, pepper, pepper pot.

LONDON'S BURNING **(4 parts)**

London's burning, London's burning,
Look yonder! Look yonder!
Fire, fire! Fire, fire!
And we have no water.

GING GANG GOOLIE (2 parts)

Ging gang goolie goolie goolie goolie watcha,
Ging gang goo, ging gang goo,
Ging gang goolie goolie goolie goolie watcha,
Ging gang goo, ging gang goo.
Heyla, heyla, sheyla,
Heyla, sheyla, heyla, hoo,
Heyla, heyla, sheyla,
Heyla sheyla heyla hoo;
Shalliwally, shalliwally, shalliwally, shalliwally,
Ompah, ompah, ompah, ompah . . . .

FRÈRE JACQUES **(4 parts)**

Frère Jacques, Frère Jacques,
Dormez-vous, dormez-vous?
Sonnez les matines, sonnez les matines,
Din, dan, don, din, dan, don.

THE BATTERED ELM TREE **(2 parts)**

From out the battered elm tree
The owl's cry we hear,
And from the distant forest,
The cuckoo answers clear:
"Cuckoo, cuckoo, cuckoo-oo-oo, oo-oo,
Cuckoo, cuckoo, cuckoo-oo-oo, oo-oo."

ANIMAL FAIR **(2 parts)**

I went to the Animal Fair,
The birds and the beasts were there,
The gay baboon by the light of the moon
Was combing his auburn hair.
The monkey fell out of his bunk,
He slid down the elephant's trunk,
The elephant sneezed and fell on his knees,
And that was the end of the monkey, monkey,
monkey, monkey . . . .

MY HAT

My hat it has three corners
Three corners has my hat;
And if it had not three corners,
It would not be my hat.

Mein hut er hat drei Ecke,
Drei Ecke hat mein hut;
Unt hat er nicht drei Ecke,
Dann er is nicht mein hut.

Mon chapeau il a trois coins,
Trois coins a mon chapeau;
Et s'il n'y a pas trois coins,
Ce n'est pas mon chapeau.

Mon chapeau il a quâtre bosses,
Quâtre bosses a mon chapeau;
Et s'il n'y a pas quâtre bosses,
Ce n'est pas mon chapeau.

AFTER THE BALL

After the ball is over,
See her take out her glass eye,
Put her false teeth in water,
Cork up her bottle of dye:
Put her false leg in the corner,
Hang up her wig on the wall—
And all that is left goes to bye-byes
After the ball.

THE BEAR WENT OVER THE MOUNTAIN

(*Tune:* For He's A Jolly Good Fellow)

The bear went over the mountain,
The bear went over the mountain,
The bear went over the mountain,
To see what he could see,
And all that he could see,
And all that he could see,
Was the other side of the mountain,
The other side of the mountain,
The other side of the mountain
Was all that he could see.

THE BELLS OF HELL

The bells of hell go ting-a-ling-a-ling,
For you but not for me:
For me the angels sing-a-ling-a-ling,
They've got the goods for me.
Oh death, where is thy sting-a-ling-a-ling,
Oh grave, thy victory?
For me the angels sing-a-ling-a-ling,
They've got the goods for me.
Hurrah, hurrah, hurrah!
I'm learning to play the harp. TWANG!

BILL SMITH

(*Tune:* Onward Christian Soldiers)

Bill Smith knows my father,
Father knows Bill Smith,
Bill Smith knows my father,
Father knows Bill Smith,
Bill Smith knows my father,
Father knows Bill Smith,
Bill Smith knows my father,
Father knows Bill Smith.

Alternative version:

Lloyd George knows my father
Father knows Lloyd George.

HIKING

(*Tune:* Pack Up Your Troubles)

Pack up your dinner in your haversack
And hike, hike, hike,
Carry all you want upon your own strong back,
And wander where you like;
Leave the road for motorcars,
The sidetrack to the bike.
So pack up your dinner in your haversack
And hike, hike, hike!

I'M A DEWDROP

(*Tune:* Clementine)

I'm a dewdrop, I'm a dewdrop,
    I'm a dewdrop, yes I am!
But I'd rather be a dewdrop
    Than a drip!

(*Variations:* teacup, mug
bloodstain, clot
crevice, crack
etc., etc., etc.).

MacTAVISH IS DEAD

(*Tune:* Irish Washerwoman)

O-o-o-oh,
MacTavish is dead and his brother don't know it,
His brother is dead and MacTavish don't know it,
They're both of them dead
And they're in the same bed,
But neither one knows that the other is dead.

NEVER LET YOUR BRACES DANGLE

Never let your braces dangle,
Never let your braces dangle;
One poor sport, he got caught
Right in the middle of a mangle.
In through the rollers he went, by gum!
Squashed flat as linoleum,
Now he's singing in Kingdom come,
"Never let your braces dangle."

SKYE WALKING SONG

Come along, come along,
Let us foot it out together;
Come along, come along,
Be it fair or stormy weather:
With the hills of Skye before us,
And the purple of the heather,
Let us sing this happy chorus—
Come along, come along.

ROW, ROW

Row, row, row your boat
Gently down the stream;
Merrily, merrily, merrily, merrily,
Life is but a dream.

Soap, soap, soap, and towel
Towel and water please,
Merrily, merrily, merrily, merrily,
Scrub your dirty knees.

ALOUETTE

Alouette, gentile Alouette,
Alouette, je te plumerai.
Je te plumerai la tête,
Je te plumerai la tête,
Et la tête—et la tête
Alouette, Alouette,
Ooooooh!
Alouette, gentile Alouette . . . . . .

(*Add:*- le bec, le nez, le dos, le cou, la bouche, etc.).

SING TOGETHER

Sing, sing together, merrily, merrily, sing,
Sing, sing together, merrily, merrily, sing,
Sing, sing, sing, sing.

OH HOW LOVELY IS THE EVENING

Oh how lovely is the evening, is the evening,
When the bells are sweetly ringing, sweetly ringing,
Ding, dong, ding, dong, ding, dong.

MORNING IS COME

Morning is come
Night is away
Rise with the sun
And welcome the day.

MERRILY, MERRILY, GREET THE MORN

Merrily, merrily greet the morn:
Cheerily, cheerily sound the horn,
Hark! to the echoes, hear them play,
O'er hill and dale and far away.

COME, FOLLOW

Come, follow, follow, follow, follow, follow, follow me!
Whither shall I follow, follow, follow,
Whither shall I follow, follow thee?
To the greenwood, to the greenwood, to the greenwood,
greenwood tree.

BLOW, PIPERS, BLOW

The Highland lads and lassies too
Are gaily drest all in their best,
To greet the gallant soldier boys
And welcome them with joyful noise.
Blow, Pipers, blow,
All the merry tunes you know.

ALL THINGS SHALL PERISH

All things shall perish from under the sky
Music alone shall live,
Music alone shall live,
Music alone shall live,
Never to die.

I USED TO BE A CUB SCOUT

I used to be a Cub Scout, and a good old Cub Scout too,
But now I've finished Cub Scouting, I don't know what to do;
I'm growing old and feeble, and I can Cub no more,
So I'm going to work my ticket if I can:
Back to Gilwell, happy land,
I'm going to work my ticket if I can.

(*Scout, Venture Scout, Scouter, Commissioner, Chief Scout*).

HOW NOW, BROWN COW

How now, brown cow,
Why are you looking so sad?
How now, brown cow,
You should be happy and glad.
Out in the meadow, where I first found you,
Thousands of other cows browsing around you.
How now, brown cow,
You should be happy and glad.

THREE BLIND MICE

Three blind mice, three blind mice,
See how they run, see how they run,
They all ran after the farmer's wife,
She cut off their tails with a carving knife,
Did you ever see such a thing in your life
As three blind mice?

BE KIND TO YOUR WEB-FOOTED FRIENDS

(*Tune:* Stars and Stripes Forever)

Be kind to your web-footed friends,
For a duck may be somebody's mother.
Be kind to your friends in the swamp,
Where the weather's always damp.

You may think that this is the end,
Well—it is!

DOWN BY THE STATION

Down by the station early in the morning,
See the little puffer billies all in a row.
See the engine driver turn the little handle,
Chug! chug! Whoo! whoo! Off we go!

DAISY, DAISY

Daisy, Daisy, give me your answer true,
I'm half crazy all for the love of you.
It won't be a stylish marriage,
I can't afford a carriage;
But you'll look sweet
Upon the seat
Of a bicycle made for two.

SONGS WITH ACTIONS

IF YOU'RE HAPPY AND YOU KNOW IT

If you're happy and you know it clap your hands,
If you're happy and you know it clap your hands.
If you're happy and you know it,
Then you really ought to show it;
If you're happy and you know it clap your hands.

If you're happy and you know it snap your fingers,
If you're happy and you know it snap your fingers.
If you're happy and you know it,
Then you really ought to show it;
If you're happy and you know it snap your fingers.

If you're happy and you know it slap your knees,
If you're happy and you know it slap your knees.
If you're happy and you know it,
Then you really ought to show it;
If you're happy and you know it slap your knees.

If you're happy and you know it stamp your feet,
If you're happy and you know it stamp your feet.
If you're happy and you know it,
Then you really ought to show it;
If you're happy and you know it stamp your feet.

If you're happy and you know it shout "Amen",
If you're happy and you know it shout "Amen".
If you're happy and you know it,
Then you really ought to show it;
If you're happy and you know it shout "A-men".

If you're happy and you know it do all five,
If you're happy and you know it do all five.
If you're happy and you know it,
Then you really ought to show it;
If you're happy and you know it do all five.

SHE'LL BE COMING ROUND THE MOUNTAIN

She'll be coming round the mountain when she comes,
(Poop, poop!)
She'll be coming round the mountain when she comes,
(Poop, poop!)
She'll be coming round the mountain, coming round the mountain,
She'll be coming round the mountain when she comes.
(Poop, poop!)

(*Chorus*) Singing I-yi yippee, yippee-yi,
Singing I-yi yippee, yippee-yi,
Singing I-yi yippee, I-yi yippee, I-yi yippee,
Yippee-yi.

She'll be riding six white horses when she comes,
(Whoa back!) . . . . . .

We'll all go down to meet her when she comes,
(Hiya babe!) . . . . . .

We'll kill the old red rooster when she comes,
(Hack, hack) . . . . . .

We'll all have chicken and dumpling when she comes,
(Yum, yum) . . . . . .

She'll be wearing her red flannel when she comes,
(Scratch, scratch) . . . . . .

RED MEN

We are Red Men wild and quaint
In our feathers and war paint:

(*Chorus*) Pow-wow, Pow-wow,
We're the tribe of the old Dun Cow;
All of us are red men,
Feathers in our head men,
Down among the dead men,
Pow-wow, Pow-wow!

Off we go at such a pace
Led by old Chief Monkey Face:

(*Chorus*) Pow-wow, Pow-wow . . . . . .

Up the sand-hills, steep as Alps,
We go hunting after scalps:

(*Chorus*) Pow-wow, Pow-wow . . . . . .

We will fight with knives and sticks,
Bows and arrows, guns and bricks:

(*Chorus*) Pow-wow, Pow-wow . . . . . .

Home we come back from the wars,
Welcomed by our red-nosed squaws:

(*Chorus*) Pow-wow, Pow-wow . . . . . .

Light the fires to warm our feet,
Kill the buffalo—cook the meat:

(*Chorus*) Pow-wow, Pow-wow . . . . . .

MY BONNIE

My Bonnie is over the ocean,
My Bonnie is over the sea,
My Bonnie is over the ocean,
Oh bring back my Bonnie to me.

(*Chorus*) Bring back, bring back, bring back my Bonnie to me, to me,
Bring back, bring back, Oh, bring back my Bonnie to me.

Oh, blow ye winds over the ocean,
Oh, blow ye winds over the sea,
Oh, blow ye winds over the ocean,
And bring back my Bonnie to me.

(*Chorus*) Bring back, bring back . . . . . .

Last night as I lay on my pillow,
Last night as I lay on my bed,
Last night as I lay on my pillow,
I dreamed that my Bonnie was dead.

(*Chorus*) Bring back, bring back . . . . . .

The winds have blown over the ocean,
The winds have blown over the sea,
The winds have blown over the ocean,
And brought back my Bonnie to me.

(*Chorus*) Bring back, bring back . . . . . .

FOLK SONGS AND SPIRITUALS

UNDER THE CHESTNUT TREE

Under the spreading chestnut tree,
When I held you on my knee,
We were happy as could be,
Under the spreading chestnut tree.

THE GRAND OLD DUKE OF YORK

The grand old Duke of York,
He had ten thousand men.
He marched them up to the top of the hill,
And he marched them down again.
And when they were up, they were up,
And when they were down, they were down,
And when they were only halfway up,
They were neither up nor down.

MICHAEL ROW THE BOAT ASHORE

(*Chorus*) Michael row the boat ashore, Alleluya,
Michael row the boat ashore, Alleluya.

Sister help to trim the sail, Alleluya,
Sister help to trim the sail, Alleluya.

(*Chorus*) Michael . . . . . .

The river Jordan is chilly and cold, Alleluya,
Chills the body but not the soul, Alleluya.

(*Chorus*) Michael . . . . . .

The river is deep and the river is wide, Alleluya,
Milk and honey on the other side, Alleluya.

(*Chorus*) Michael . . . . . .

ONE MORE RIVER

Old Noah once he built the ark,
There's one more river to cross.
And patched it up with hickory bark,
There's one more river to cross.

(*Chorus*) One more river
And that's the river of Jordan,
One more river
There's one more river to cross.

He went to work to load his stock,
He anchored the ark with a great big rock.

(*Chorus*) One more river . . . . . .

The animals went in one by one,
The elephant chewing a caraway bun.

(*Chorus*) One more river . . . . . .

The animals went in two by two,
The rhinoceros and the kangaroo.

(*Chorus*) One more river . . . . . .

The animals went in three by three,
The bear, the flea, and the bumble bee.
(*Chorus*) One more river . . . . . .

The animals went in four by four,
The great hippopotamus got stuck in the door.
(*Chorus*) One more river . . . . . .

The animals went in five by five,
With packing trunks they did arrive.
(*Chorus*) One more river . . . . . .

The animals went in six by six,
The hyena laughed at the monkey's tricks.
(*Chorus*) One more river . . . . . .

The animals went in seven by seven,
Said the ant to the elephant, "Who are you shovin'?"
(*Chorus*) One more river . . . . . .

The animals went in eight by eight,
They came with a rush because it was late.
(*Chorus*) One more river . . . . . .

The animals went in nine by nine,
Old Noah shouted: "Cut that line".
(*Chorus*) One more river . . . . . .

The animals went in ten by ten,
The ark she blowed her whistle then.
(*Chorus*) One more river . . . . . .

And then the voyage did begin,
Old Noah pulled the gang-plank in.
(*Chorus*) One more river . . . . . .

They never knew where they were at,
Till the ark it bumped on Ararat.
(*Chorus*) One more river . . . . . .

The ark it landed high and dry,
The baboon kissed the cow good-bye.
(*Chorus*) One more river . . . . . .

Now all remember well the text,
To be continued in our next.
(*Chorus*) One more river . . . . . .

KILLARNEY

By Killarney's lakes and fells,
Emerald isles and winding bays,
Mountain paths and woodland dells,
Mem'ry ever fondly strays.
Bounteous nature loves all lands:
Beauty wanders ev'rywhere.
Footprints leaves on many strands,
But her home is surely there.
Angels fold their wings and rest
In that Eden of the West,
Beauty's home Killarney,
Heav'ns reflex, Killarney.

HOME ON THE RANGE

Oh, give me a home where the buffaloes roam,
Where the deer and the antelopes play.
There seldom is heard a discouraging word,
And the sky is not cloudy all day.

(*Chorus*) Home, home on the range,
Where the deer and the antelopes play.
There seldom is heard a discouraging word,
And the sky is not cloudy all day.

Yes, give me the gleam of the swift mountain stream,
And the place where no hurricanes blow.
Oh, give me the park where the prairie dogs bark,
And the mountains all covered with snow.

(*Chorus*) Home, home . . . . . .

Oh, give me the hills and the ring of the drills,
And the rich silver ore in the ground.
Yes, give me the gulch where the miner can sluice,
And the bright yellow gold can be found.

(*Chorus*) Home, home . . . . . .

Oh, give me the steed and the gun that I need
To shoot game for my own cabin home.
Then give me the camp where the fire is the lamp,
And the wild rocky mountains to roam.

(*Chorus*) Home, home . . . . . .

Oh, give me the mine where the prospectors find
The gold in its own native land.
And the hot springs below where the sick people go,
And the camp on the banks of the Grand.

(*Chorus*) Home, home . . . . . .

Yes, give me the home where the prospectors roam,
There business is always alive.
In those wild western hills midst the ring of the drills,
Oh, there let me live till I die.

(*Chorus*) Home, home . . . . . .

COCKLES AND MUSSELS

In Dublin's fair city,
Where the girls are so pretty,
I first set my eyes on sweet Molly Malone,
And she wheel'd her wheel-barrow
Thro' streets broad and narrow,
Crying "Cockles and Mussels! Alive a-live-o!"

(*Chorus*) A-live, a-live-o!
A-live, a-live-o!
Crying Cockles and Mussels
A-live, a-live-o!

She was a fishmonger,
But sure 'twas no wonder,
For so were her father and mother before,
And they each wheel'd their barrow
Thro' streets broad and narrow,
Crying "Cockles and Mussels! A-live, a-live-o!"

(*Chorus*) A-live, a-live-o! . . . . . .

She died of a fever,
And no one could save her,
And that was the end of sweet Molly Malone;
But her ghost wheels a barrow,
Thro' streets broad and narrow,
Crying "Cockles and Mussels! A-live, a-live-o!"

(*Chorus*) A-live, a-live-o! . . . . . .

SHENANDOAH

Oh Shenandoah, I long to hear you,
And see your rolling river,
Oh Shenandoah, I long to hear you,
Away, we're bound away, 'cross the wide Missouri.

I long to see your smiling valley,
And hear your rolling river,
I long to see your smiling valley,
Away, we're bound away, 'cross the wide Missouri.

'Tis seven long years since last I saw thee,
And heard your rolling river,
'Tis seven long years since last I saw thee,
Away, we're bound to go, 'cross the wide Missouri.

When first I took a rambling notion,
To leave your rolling river,
To sail across the briny ocean,
Away, we're bound away, 'cross the wide Missouri.

THE ROAD TO THE ISLES

A far croonin' is pullin' me away
As tak' I wi' my cromak to the road,
It's the far Coolins that are puttin' love on me
As step I wi' the sunlight for my load.

(*Chorus*) Sure, by Tummel and Loch Rannoch and
Lochaber I will go,
By heather tracks wi' heaven in their wiles;
If you're thinking in your inner heart that
braggart's in my step
You've never smelt the tangle o' the Isles.
Oh, the far Coolins are puttin' love on me
As step I wi' my cromak to the Isles.

It's by Sheil water that the track is to the West,
By Aillort and by Morar to the sea;
It's the cool tresses I am thinkin' o' for pluck,
And bracken for a wink on Mother's knee.

(*Chorus*) Sure, by Tummel . . . . . .

It's the Blue Islands that are pullin' me away,
Their laughter puts the leap upon the lame;
It's the Blue Islands from the Skerries to the Lews,
Wi' heather honey taste upon each name.

(*Chorus*) Sure, by Tummel . . . . . .

JOHNNY COME DOWN TO THE HILO

I never seen the like since I was born,
When a big buck nigger with seaboots on, says:

(*Chorus*) Johnny come down to Hilo, poor old man,
Oh wake her, Oh shake her, oh
Wake dat girl wid de blue dress on
When Johnny comes down to Hilo,
Poor old man.

I love a little girl across the sea,
She's a Badian beauty and she says to me, "Oh":

(*Chorus*) Johnny come down . . . . . .

Was you ever down in Mobile Bay?
Where they sow the cotton on a summer day:

(*Chorus*) Johnny come down . . . . . .

Did you ever see the old plantation boss,
And the long-tailed filly and the big black hoss?

(*Chorus*) Johnny come down . . . . . .

I never seen the like since I was born,
When a big buck nigger with seaboots on, says:

(*Chorus*) Johnny come down . . . . . .

A-ROVING

In Plymouth town there lived a maid,
Mark well what I do say,
In Plymouth town there lived a maid,
And she was mistress of her trade,
I'll go no more a-roving with you, fair maid.

(*Chorus*) A-Roving, A-Roving, since Roving's been my ruin.
I'll go no more A-Roving with you, fair maid.

I put my arm around her waist,
Mark well what I do say,
I put my arm around her waist,
She said "Young man, you're in great haste!"
I'll go no more a-roving with you, fair maid.

(*Chorus*) A-Roving . . . . . .

I took that girl upon my knee,
Mark well what I do say,
I took that girl upon my knee
Said she, "Young man, you're rather free!"
I'll go no more a-roving with you, fair maid.

(*Chorus*) A-Roving . . . . . .

COME, LASSES AND LADS

Come, lasses and lads, get leave of your dads,
And away to the Maypole high,
For ev'ry fair has a sweetheart there,
And the fiddlers standing by.
For Willie shall dance with Jane,
And Johnny has got his Joan,
To trip it, trip it, trip it, trip it,
Trip it up and down.

"You're out," says Dick, "Not I" says Nick,
"'Twas the fiddler play'd it wrong,"
"'Tis true," says Hugh, and so says Sue,
And so says ev'ry one.
The fiddler then began
To play the tune again,
And ev'ry girl did trip it, trip it,
Trip it to the men.

Then after an hour they went to a bower,
And play'd for ale and cakes;
And kisses too—until they were due,
The lasses held the stakes.
The girls did then begin
To quarrel with the men,
And bade them take their kisses back,
And give them their own again.

"Good-night," says Harry, "Good-night," says Mary,
"Good-night," says Poll to John;
"Good-night," says Sue to her sweetheart Hugh,
"Good-night," says ev'ry one.
Some walk'd and some did run,
Some loiter'd on the way,
And bound themselves by kisses twelve,
To meet next holiday.

ROCK MY SOUL

Rock my soul in the bosom of Abraham,
Rock my soul in the bosom of Abraham,
Rock my soul in the bosom of Abraham,
O rock-a-my soul.

So high I can't get over it,
So high I can't get over it,
So high I can't get over it,
O rock-a-my soul.

So low I can't get under it,
So low I can't get under it,
So low I can't get under it,
O rock-a-my soul.

So wide I can't get round of it,
So wide I can't get round of it,
So wide I can't get round of it,
O rock-a-my soul.

WHEN I FIRST CAME TO THIS LAND

When I first came to this land
I was not a wealthy man,
So I got myself a shack,
I did all I could.

And I called my shack,
Break my back.
I did all I could.

When I first came to this land,
I was not a wealthy man,
So I got myself a cow,
I did all I could.

And I called my cow
No milk now,
And I called my shack
Break my back,
I did all I could.

When I first came to this land
I was not a wealthy man,
So I got myself a hen,
And I called my hen . . .

Now and then,
And I called my cow
No milk now,
And I called my shack
Break my back,
I did all I could.

When I first came to this land
I was not a wealthy man,
So I got myself a donkey,
And I called my donkey . . . .

Horse gone wonkey,
And I called my cow
No Milk now,
And I called my shack
Break my back,
I did all I could.

When I first came to this land
I was not a wealthy man,
So I got myself a wife,
And I called my wife . . . .

Run for your life,
And I called my donkey
Horse gone wonkey,
And I called my shack
Break my back,
I did all I could.

When I first came to this land
I was not a wealthy man,
So I got myself a son,
And I called my son . . . . .

My work done,
And I called my wife
Run for your life,
And I called my donkey
Horse gone wonkey,
And I called my shack
Break my back.

But the land was sweet and good,
I did all I could.

WIDDICOMBE FAIR

Tom Pearse, Tom Pearse lend me your grey mare,
All along, down along, out along lee;
For I want to go to Widdicombe Fair,

(*Chorus*) Wi' Bill Brewer, Jan Stewer, Peter Gurney,
Peter Davy, Dan'l Whiddon, Harry Hawe,
Old Uncle Tom Cobleigh and all,
Old Uncle Tom Cobleigh and all.

And when shall I see again my grey mare?
All along, down along, out along lee;
By Friday soon, or Saturday noon,

(*Chorus*) Wi' Bill Brewer . . . . . .

Then Friday came and Saturday noon,
All along, down along, out along lee;
But Tom Pearse's old mare hath not trotted home,

(*Chorus*) Wi' Bill Brewer . . . . . .

So Tom Pearse he got up to the top of the hill,
All along, down along, out along lee;
And he seed his old mare down a-making her will,

(*Chorus*) Wi' Bill Brewer . . . . . .

So Tom Pearse's old grey mare her took sick and died,
All along, down along, out along lee;
And Tom he sat down on a stone and he cried,

(*Chorus*) Wi' Bill Brewer . . . . . .

But this isn't the end of this shocking affair,
All along, down along, out along lee;
Nor, though they be dead, of the horrid career,

(*Chorus*) Wi' Bill Brewer . . . . . .

When the wind whistles cold on the moor of a night,
All along, down along, out along lee;
Tom Pearse's old mare doth appear gashly white,

(*Chorus*) Wi' Bill Brewer . . . . . .

And all the long night be heard skirling and groans,
All along, down along, out along lee;
From Tom Pearse's old mare in her rattling bones,

(*Chorus*) And from Bill Brewer . . . . . .

GO TELL IT ON THE MOUNTAIN

When I was a sinner, I prayed both night and day;
I asked my Lord to help me and He showed me the way.

(*Chorus*) Go tell it on the mountain,
Over the hills and everywhere,
Go tell it on the mountain,
That Jesus Christ is born.

When I was a seeker, I sought both night and day;
I asked my Lord to help me, and He taught me to pray.

(*Chorus*) Go tell it on the mountain . . . . . .

He made me a watchman upon the city wall;
And if I am a Christian, I am the least of all.

(*Chorus*) Go tell it on the mountain . . . . . .

SWORD AND SHIELD

Gonna lay down my sword and shield, down by the riverside,
Down by the riverside, down by the riverside.
Gonna lay down my sword and shield, down by the riverside,
Gonna study war no more.

(*Chorus*) I ain't gonna study war no more
I ain't gonna study war no more
I ain't gonna study war no more
I ain't gonna study war no more
I ain't gonna study war no more
I ain't gonna study war no more.

Gonna walk with the Prince of Peace, down by the riverside,
Down by the riverside, down by the riverside.
Gonna walk with the Prince of Peace, down by the riverside,
Gonna study war no more.

(*Chorus*) I ain't gonna study war no more . . . . . .

Gonna shake hands round the world, down by the riverside,
Down by the riverside, down by the riverside.
Gonna shake hands round the world, down by the riverside,
Gonna study war no more.

(*Chorus*) I ain't gonna study war no more . . . . . .

THIS LITTLE LIGHT OF MINE

The light that shines in the light of love,
Lights the darkness from above
It shines on me and it shines on you
And shows what the power of Love can do,
I'm gonna shine my light both far and near,
I'm gonna shine my light both bright and clear
Where there's a dark corner in this land
I'm gonna let my little light shine.

(*Chorus*) This little light of mine, I'm gonna let it shine,
This little light of mine, I'm gonna let it shine,
This little light of mine, I'm gonna let it shine,
Let it shine, let it shine, let it shine.

On Monday He gave me the gift of love,
Tuesday peace came from above;
On Wednesday He told me to have more faith
On Thursday He gave me a little more grace
Friday He told me just to watch and pray,
Saturday He told me just what to say;
On Sunday He gave me the power divine,
To let my little light shine.

(*Chorus*) This little light of mine . . . . . .

HE'S GOT THE WHOLE WORLD

He's got the whole world in His hand,
He's got the whole wide world in His hand,
He's got the whole world in His hand,
He's got the whole world in His hand.

He's got the little bitty baby in His hand,
He's got the little bitty baby in His hand,
He's got the little bitty baby in His hand,
He's got the whole world in His hand.

He's got you and me brother, in His hand,
He's got you and me brother, in His hand,
He's got you and me brother, in His hand,
He's got the whole world in His hand.

He's got you and me sister, in His hand,
He's got you and me sister, in His hand,
He's got you and me sister, in His hand,
He's got the whole world in His hand.

He's got everybody here, in His hand,
He's got everybody here, in His hand,
He's got everybody here, in His hand,
He's got the whole world in His hand.

LORD OF THE DANCE

I danced in the morning, when the world was begun,
And I danced in the moon and the stars and the sun;
And I came down from heaven and I danced on the earth,
At Bethlehem I had my birth.

(*Chorus*) Dance then, wherever you may be,
I am the Lord of the Dance said he,
And I'll lead you all wherever you may be,
And I'll lead you all in the Dance said he.

I danced for the scribe and the pharisee,
But they would not dance and they wouldn't follow me.
I danced for the fishermen, for James and John—
They came with me and the dance went on.

(*Chorus*) Dance then . . . . . .

I danced on the Sabbath and I cured the lame;
The holy people said it was a shame,
They whipped and they stripped and they hung me on high
And they left me there on a cross to die.

(*Chorus*) Dance then . . . . . .

I danced on a Friday when the sky turned black;
It's hard to dance with the devil on your back.
They buried my body and they thought I'd gone;
But I am the dance and I still go on.

(*Chorus*) Dance then . . . . . .

They cut me down and I leapt up high;
I am the life that'll never, never die.
I'll live in you if you'll live in me;
I am the Lord of the Dance, said he.

(*Chorus*) Dance then . . . . . .

I KNOW WHERE I'M GOIN'

I know where I'm goin',
And I know who's goin' with me.
I know who I love,
But my dear knows who I'll marry.

I'll wear stockings of silk,
And shoes of bright green leather,
Combs to buckle my hair,
And a ring for every finger.

Feather beds are soft,
And painted rooms are bonny,
But I would trade them all,
For my handsome, winsome Johnny.

Some say he's dark,
But I say he's bonny,
Fairest of them all
Is my handsome, winsome, Johnny.

GREENSLEEVES

Alas, my love you do me wrong
To treat me so discourteously.
And I have loved you so long,
Delighting in your company.

(*Chorus*) Greensleeves was all my joy.
Greensleeves was my delight.
Greensleeves was my heart of gold,
And who but Lady Greensleeves.

THE BLUE-TAIL FLY

When I was young, I used to wait
Upon old Master and pass his plate,
And fetch the bottle when he got dry,
And brush away the blue-tail fly.

(*Chorus*) Jimmie Crack Corn, and I don't care,
Jimmie Crack Corn, and I don't care,
Jimmie Crack Corn, and I don't care,
My Master's gone away.

And when he'd ride in the afternoon,
I'd follow with a hickory broom,
The pony being very shy
Got bitten by a blue-tailed fly.

(*Chorus*) Jimmie Crack . . . . . .

One day he rode around the farm
The flies so numerous they did swarm,
One chanced to bite him on the thigh
The devil take the blue-tail fly.

(*Chorus*) Jimmie Crack . . . . . .

The pony run, he jump, he pitch,
He threw old Master in a ditch,
He died and the jury wondered why
The verdict was the blue-tailed fly.

(*Chorus*) Jimmie Crack . . . . . .

They laid him under a 'simmon tree,
His epitaph is there to see:
"Beneath this stone I'm forced to lie
A victim of the blue-tail fly."

(*Chorus*) Jimmie Crack . . . . . .

JOSHUA FOUGHT THE BATTLE OF JERICHO

You can talk about your king
Of Gideon,
You can talk about your man of Saul,
There's none like good cld Joshua,
At the battle of Jericho that morning.

(*Chorus*) Joshua fought the battle of Jericho,
Jericho, Jericho,
Joshua fought the battle of Jericho,
And the walls came tumbling down.

Up to the walls of Jericho
He marched with spear in hand
"Go blow them horns," old Joshua cried,
"Cause the battle is in my hand."

(*Chorus*) Joshua fought . . . . . .

Then the lamb ram horns begin to blow
Trumpets begin to sound,
Joshua commanded the children to shout
And the walls came tumbling down that morning.

(*Chorus*) Joshua fought . . . . . .

SKIP TO MY LOU

Lost my partner, what'll I do,
Lost my partner, what'll I do,
Lost my partner, what'll I do,
Skip to My Lou, my darling.

(*Chorus*) Lou, Lou, Skip to My Lou,
Lou, Lou, Skip to My Lou,
Lou, Lou, Skip to My Lou,
Skip to My Lou, my darling.

I'll get another one, prettier than you,
I'll get another one, prettier than you,
I'll get another one, prettier than you,
Skip to My Lou, my darling.

(*Chorus*) Lou, Lou . . . . . .

Gone again, skip to My Lou,
Gone again, skip to My Lou,
Gone again, skip to My Lou,
Skip to My Lou, my darling.

(*Chorus*) Lou, Lou . . . . . .

Fly's in the buttermilk, shoo, shoo, shoo,
Fly's in the buttermilk, shoo, shoo, shoo,
Fly's in the buttermilk, shoo, shoo, shoo,
Skip to My Lou, my darling.

(*Chorus*) Lou, Lou . . . . . .

A little red wagon, painted blue,
A little red wagon, painted blue,
A little red wagon, painted blue,
Skip to My Lou, my darling.

(*Chorus*) Lou, Lou . . . . . .

DIXIE

I wish I was in the land of cotton,
Old times there are not forgotten;
Look away! Look away! Look away! Dixie Land.
In Dixie Land where I was born in,
Early on one frosty mornin',
Look away! Look away! Look away! Dixie Land.

(*Chorus*) Then I wish I was in Dixie, Hooray, Hooray!
In Dixie Land I'll take my stand to live and die in Dixie,
Away, away, away down south in Dixie,
Away, away, away down south in Dixie.

CLOSING SONGS

GOD SAVE THE QUEEN

God save our gracious Queen,
Long live our noble Queen,
God save the Queen.
Send her victorious,
Happy and glorious,
Long to reign over us,
God save the Queen.

Thy choicest gifts in store,
On her be pleased to pour,
Long may she reign.
May she defend our laws,
And ever give us cause
To sing with heart and voice,
God save the Queen.

GOOD - BYE - EE!

Good-bye-ee! good-bye-ee!
Wipe the tear, baby dear, from your eye-ee.
Tho' it's hard to part, I know,
I'll be tickled to death to go.
Don't cry-ee! Don't sigh-ee!
There's a silver lining in the sky-ee.
Bonsoir, old thing! Cheerio! Chin-chin!
Nah-poo! Toodle-oo! Good-bye-ee!

GOOD-NIGHT, LADIES

Good-night, ladies,
Good-night, ladies,
Good-night, ladies,
We're going to leave you now.

Merrily we roll along, roll along, roll along,
Merrily we roll along, o'er the dark blue sea.

(*Note: Patrol names can be substituted for the word 'ladies'*).

TILL WE MEET AGAIN

By the camp-fire's fading light
We have met in comradeship tonight,
And above, the whispering trees
Guard our many memories;
So before we close our eyes in sleep
We will pledge each other that we keep
Scouting memories long and deep,
Till we meet again.

TAPS

(*Tune:* Bugle Call, Lights Out)

Day is done, gone the sun
From the lake, from the hills, from the sky,
All is well, safely rest,
God is nigh.

Fading light, dims the sight,
And a star gems the sky, gleaming bright,
From afar, drawing night,
Falls the night.

O COME AND GO WITH ME

O come and go with me, Alleluya,
To my Father's house, Alleluya,
To my Father's house, Alleluya,
To my Father's house.
O come and go with me, Alleluya,
To my Father's house,
Where there's peace, peace, peace.

There's sweet communion there, Alleluya,
In my Father's house, Alleluya,
In my Father's house, Alleluya,
In my Father's house.
There's sweet communion there, Alleluya,
In my Father's house,
Where there's peace, peace, peace.

There'll be no parting there, Alleluya,
In my Father's house, Alleluya,
In my Father's house, Alleluya,
In my Father's house.
There'll be no parting there, Alleluya,
Where there's peace, peace, peace.

CANADIAN TAPS

Each camp-fire lights anew
The flame of friendship true;
The joy we've had in knowing you
Will last the whole year through.

CAMP FIRE

(*Tune:* The Bells of St. Mary's)

The embers of camp-fire
Are now slowly dying,
The birds and the woodfolk
Are gone to their rest,
The stars they are shining,
Their light gleaming o'er us,
O God of Nature, grant to us
A perfect rest.

GOOD-NIGHT TO YOU ALL

Good-night to you all and sweet be your sleep,
May angels around you their vigil keep
Good-night, good-night, good-night, good-night.

ADIEU

(*Tune:* Tavern In The Town)

Our camp is over, to the town, to the town,
We must away and settle down, settle down,
And bid farewell to mountain and to sea,
And life out of doors that is so free.

(*Chorus*) Fare thee well, for I must leave three,
Do not let the parting grieve thee,
And remember that the best of friends must
part, must part.
Adieu, adieu, kind friends adieu, adieu, adieu,
I can no longer stay with you, stay with you,
I'll hang my harp on a weeping willow tree,
And may the world go well with three.

We've ranged the moors and hills together, hills together,
Faced all sorts of rain and sunny weather, sunny weather,
And now where'er our future path may lead,
Through storm or shine we'll wish "God speed".

(*Chorus*) Fare three well . . . . . .

And if our road were long and dusty, long and dusty,
Our feet kept time to song so lusty, song so lusty,
That our ears still ring with the swinging tuneful jaunt,
While ghosts of jokes our memories haunt.

(*Chorus*) Fare three well . . . . . .

ALL THROUGH THE NIGHT

While the moon her watch is keeping,
All through the night,
While the weary world is sleeping,
All through the night,
O'er my bosom gently stealing,
Visions of delight revealing,
Breathes a pure and holy feeling,
All through the night.

Love, to thee my thoughts are turning,
All through the night,
All for thee my heart is yearning,
All through the night,
Though sad fate our lives may sever,
Parting will not last for ever,
There's a hope that leaves me never,
All through the night.

AMAZING GRACE

Amazing grace! How sweet the sound
That saved a wretch like me!
I once was lost, but now am found,
Was blind, but now I see.

'Twas grace that taught my heart to fear
And grace my fears relieved;
How precious did that grace appear
The hour I first believed.

Thro' many dangers, toils and snares,
I have already come;
'Tis grace hath brought me safe thus far
And grace will lead me home.

The Lord has promised good to me,
His word my hope secures;
He will my shield and portion be
As long as life endures.

KUM BA YAH

Kum ba yah, my Lord, Kum ba yah,
Kum ba yah, my Lord, Kum ba yah,
Kum ba yah, my Lord, Kum ba yah,
Oh Lord, Kum ba yah.

Someone's singing Lord, Kum ba yah,
Someone's singing Lord, Kum ba yah,
Someone's singing Lord, Kum ba yah,
Oh Lord, Kum ba yah.

Someone's crying Lord, Kum ba yah,
Someone's crying Lord, Kum ba yah,
Someone's crying Lord, Kum ba yah,
Oh Lord, Kum ba yah.

Someone's praying Lord, Kum ba yah,
Someone's praying Lord, Kum ba yah,
Someone's praying Lord, Kum ba yah,
Oh Lord, Kum ba yah.

Someone's dying Lord, Kum ba yah,
Someone's dying Lord, Kum ba yah,
Someone's dying Lord, Kum ba yah,
Oh Lord, Kum ba yah.

GOOD NIGHT SONG

(*Tune:* Auld Lang Syne)

The time has come to say so-long,
We will be upon our way,
The camp-fire light is dying now,
At the end of a perfect day.

We give our thanks for glory days,
For blessings from above,
The Scouting game, our Founder's fame,
And the Movement that we love.

So raise your voices high my lads,
As now we say good night,
We'll keep the camp-fire burning on,
In our hearts forever bright.

Good cheer, God bless, and cheerio,
We say to one another,
And go upon our chosen way,
Every one of us a brother.

WERE YOU THERE?

Were you there when they crucified my Lord?
Were you there when they crucified my Lord?
Oh—sometimes it causes me to tremble, tremble, tremble;
Were you there when they crucified my Lord?
Were you there when they nailed Him to the tree?
Were you there when they pierced Him in the side?
Were you there when the sun refused to shine?
Were you there when they laid Him in the tomb?
Were you there when He rose from out the tomb?

AULD LANG SYNE

Should auld acquaintance be forgot,
And never bro't to mind?
Should auld acquaintance be forgot
And days of auld lang syne?

(*Chorus*) For auld lang syne, my dear,
For auld lang syne;
We'll tak' a cup o' kindness yet
For the sake of auld lang syne.

And here's a hand, my trusty friend,
And gi'es a hand o' thine;
We'll tak' a cup o' kindness yet,
For auld lang syne.

(*Chorus*) For auld lang syne . . . . . .

BATTLE HYMN OF THE REPUBLIC

Mine eyes have seen the glory of the coming of the Lord;
He is trampling out the vintage where the grapes of wrath are stored;
He hath loosed the fateful lightning of His terrible swift sword;
His truth is marching on.

(*Chorus*) Glory, glory! Hallelujah!
Glory, glory! Hallelujah!
Glory, glory! Hallelujah!
His truth is marching on.

I have seen Him in the watchfires of a hundred circling camps;
They have builded Him an altar in the evening dews and damps;
I can read His righteous sentence by the dim and flaring lamps;
His day is marching on.

(*Chorus*) Glory, glory . . . . . .

He has sounded forth the trumpet that shall never call retreat;
He is sifting out the hearts of men before His judgement seat;
Oh, be swift, my soul, to answer Him! be jubilant, my feet!
Our God is marching on.

(*Chorus*) Glory, glory . . . . . .

In the beauty of the lilies Christ was born across the sea
With a glory in his bosum that transfigures you and me.
As he died to make men holy, let us die to make men free.
Whilst God is marching on.

(*Chorus*) Glory, glory . . . . . .